Your Access Course – be

Updated .

By Dan Berry

Contents

# Who is this book for?

If you are nineteen or over, without the qualifications needed to go to university, this book is for you. You will discover how to find the Access to Higher Education course that is right for you. You will get suggestions on how to hit the ground running when the course starts. For most of the book I am just going to say "Access" rather than the full title.

You will learn the strange language of credits, levels, units, modules, criteria and grades. You want to succeed so there is information on how to give yourself the best chance – and how to deal with setbacks. You will share hours daily with a set of people with the same aim as you. But being people they can be quirky. There are hints on relationships. Throughout the book there are also hints on how to deal with some of the problems.

It has been my privilege to work with Access learners for almost quarter of a century. 98% of my current year's students have completed their courses and will be off to university in just a few weeks. I have put this book together to answer the commonest questions you ask. I have produced these suggestions simply by drawing on my everyday experiences teaching the most enthusiastic, committed and utterly brilliant set of students anyone could wish to share their working hours with.

Education and education funding is always changing, so this new edition includes the latest changes to Access courses, UCAS points and also information about course costs, loans and so on.

I hope you find it a useful companion over the next few months. Hold tight and enjoy your journey!

Dan Berry.

# Choosing your Access Course

Your search for entry to university is like asking 3 different people in a strange town for directions. You get a lot of arm waving in a very authoritative manner. It's only later, bumping down a farm track in the middle of nowhere it dawns that you are on a wild goose chase. They didn't have a clue. Lord Sugar might couch it more strongly.

Your first inkling about Access might have come from a university, a friend, the TV, UCAS or the internet. You are hungry for more information. To begin, you need to do some serious research.

**First** of all, what is your eventual goal after your degree? Is it nursing? Midwifery? Social work? Something biological… or chemistry related, or physics? If you aren't sure- hold it right now. Find out more about your interest area-what are the career prospects? Look on the internet. Get in touch with your local college's Careers Adviser-they will be able to give you a feel for the various choices open to you.

**Secondly**, what are your university choices? The more the merrier, within reason. Remember, rejection for a particular university place may simply be due to number restrictions, not your qualities as a student. Are you able to study the other side or end of the country? Or do you have personal commitments meaning you must study within commuting distance?

Case Study

Guy was married with two children aged 7 and 12. He had always been fascinated by evolution and wanted to study Palaeobiology as a single subject. At that time there were four universities that met his personal requirements which included good dyslexia support. All four were over four hours journey time away. Before he started the Access course he discussed the options with his wife and children. They agreed that if he got a place they would move closer to the university. Guy was offered places at two of the universities, so in October they spent a couple of weekends looking at the surrounding areas of each and the availability of housing and schools.

By Easter it became obvious he was going to pass the course with the required grades, so they started making all the arrangements to move at the beginning of summer.

Guy was unusual. His very tight knit family made a very tough decision. For every Guy there are many hundreds of students who have much more choice within reasonable travelling time.

As a tutor I have noticed an increased number of students willing to relocate. Most are in the early 20s single, unattached group. Nonetheless, most Access students remain restricted in their choices of university due to home ties.

**Thirdly**, research the entry requirements of all the universities on your shortlist. Do it right away, when you have finished this chapter. A small number of universities are not actively seeking mature students (though they won't admit to it). Don't waste your time with them. They will ask for impossibly high requirements and then if you achieve them, hunt round for some way to renege on their offer. Others (including some at Oxford and Cambridge) are much more amenable.

Case Study

Ailsa had come to the UK from Africa several years before. Ailsa wanted to study pharmacology. Although she already had the equivalent of good GCSE and A level qualifications from her home country, these were not acceptable for entry to UK universities. Ailsa checked the university literature and saw that Access to HE: Science courses were considered, so she enrolled on one locally. She ignored universities which seemed to concentrate on A level students and applied for a shortlist of four universities. She was invited to interviews at two of them and offered a place at one. She completed the course with flying colours, but when she told her intended university they withdrew their offer on the basis she did not have UK English at GCSE level.

If Ailsa had spoken to the university before she even started the Access course she could have seen this coming and discussed the matter with them. Happily, the university – after she appealed – reconsidered and reluctantly confirmed a place. Ailsa is now working in pharmacological research on her post graduate degree.

So find out if they want specific subjects covered in your Access course. What are their entry requirements... all Distinctions? Just pass the course? Don't just rely on their website course details; speak to someone at the university. At the very least speak to the Admissions Tutor, but better still speak to the Course Tutor/Leader. Most importantly get their name and make a written note of your conversation, with the date and time. Incidentally, 2017 is a landmark year in that Access courses will now attract UCAS points just like A levels, Though most universities will still be using your credit profile in their offers, a small number will stipulate UCAS points. There's a useful link at https://www.ucas.com/ucas/tariff-calculator showing how to calculate the implications of this for you.

You may be curling your toes in horror at the idea of speaking to these august academics. No problem-the good news is you don't have to speak to anyone to do this…. Send them an email, then you have it in writing.

**Fourthly**, find out where you can enrol on an Access course that meets all the requirements you have already researched. That's ALL the requirements. If something is missing, be very wary of bland reassurances from the person you see at the college. If in doubt, try somewhere else. The vast majority of interviewing tutors are highly experienced in the Access world and will not be afraid to send you elsewhere. Just sometimes you will meet a less experienced, enthusiastic tutor who wants to be salesperson of the year. If you have done your research properly, be content to stick to your guns and walk away!

**Finally** - Is it just pie in the sky? You need to be cruel to be kind to yourself. How many jobs are available in that career? What's the pay like? What are the chances for progression? Will the jobs disappear in the near future? Do some serious research for this big step in your life. Use the internet, libraries and talk to people that know.

Quite a few years ago working in a Pathology Laboratory was a popular goal for students. But now, most of the work isn't done by white coated science graduate technicians, it is automated. Samples go in one end, results come out the other. Many of those highly qualified students are now doing something else. Fishing for instance.

A similar thing happened in Forensic Science. Fired up by various TV series, thousands of students up and down the country wanted to get a Forensic Science degree and solve crimes. Preferably juicy murders.

Universities got fired up too. Particularly by the alluring prospect of more student income. More and more universities set up Forensic Science degree courses. Then financial stringencies struck. The Forensic Science service was set up for reform by the government of the day. The number of degree opportunities declined. A lot of the work has been automated. There is tough competition for university places, and after that for a reduced number of high up jobs.

Case Study

Since leaving school, Sue had done courses in hairdressing, massage, sports training as well as having a family. At one time she was drawn to training to become a paramedic. Her courses had fired up her interest in the human body to the extent she considered a career in physiotherapy. Despite knowing the scarcity of physiotherapy degree places she decided to have a go anyway.

Out of applications to five universities she got no offers at all. That's a big fat zero. Sue was naturally disappointed but picked herself up and immediately started exploring her previous interest – becoming a paramedic. Her enquiries with universities indicated that places were quite tricky. Then she discovered that there was a scheme in a neighbouring ambulance service for training paramedics on the job. Instead of a three year degree with all the attendant costs she could now train over a shorter period and get a training salary. They just wanted her to pass her Access course which included human physiology. An additional plus was that she wouldn't need to relocate.

Do some more research. Is your prospective career subject to political interference? For instance take careers in nursing, midwifery, probation service and teaching. All very rewarding safe enough, secure jobs you would think. Periodically governments of whatever colour will impose cuts on recruitment- often through limiting the number of places universities can offer by one means or another.

# Can I hack it?

Great! So you have researched your future career realistically. You have contacted universities and established their specific entry requirements. Your local college offers an Access course that exactly meets the requirements.

Your other self now starts wagging a finger at you.

"The teachers at school always told me I wasn't an academic".

"I failed before so what's changed?"

"Get real!"

"Can I seriously get ready for university with eight months study?"

The list is endless. But ask any experienced Access tutor and they will tell you that something weird and rather wonderful happens when you leave school for a few years. Maybe get a job, maybe raise a family, maybe travel round a bit. Look at these students' experiences:

> Christine was a lively 20 year old who left school without taking GCSE's. "I don't know why I found school such a deal", she said three weeks into the course. "Everything seems to make so much more sense now".

> Ellie had nurtured a lifelong ambition to be a midwife-but the time had never been right. At 46 years old, she enrolled on an Access to HE: Midwifery course. "But Ellie, they won't accept a 47 year old for a midwifery degree; you'll be 50 when you graduate and become registered!" said friends. "They" did take her – snapped her up at one of the top midwifery institutions. She did qualify and is now fulfilling her life's dream.

> Tony was made redundant from the IT business at 56 years old. On the employment scrapheap. Too old for another job in software.

He picked himself up from the floor - he had always been fascinated by chemistry. You've guessed it; he took an Access course and applied to university. "Tony you're way too old," joked friends. He got a place and got his degree.

So turn your back on negative you and trust in yourself. Just for once listen to positive you rather than negative you. Something in your brain has told you that you are ready for Access, ready for university, ready for a new direction. Listen - and believe in yourself.

Brian Tracy is a well-known inspirational speaker. One of his quotes is, "It's not 'what you believe you are' but 'what you believe ... you are'". Trust your positive instinct.

That's not to say you can just blithely sail into the sunset without preparation. The next chapter outlines things to consider before you get your wallet out.

# Banana skins, monsters and sirens

Some of the Access to Teaching group were sitting around on a cold dark January afternoon. They were having a pretty broody conversation. One of them - Ian - had just lost his part time job and was short of cash. I noticed that Nick was just sitting back listening, but not joining in the general moaning about money.

Nick was 28 and aiming at secondary school teaching. He was a single dad, widowed, with 2 youngsters. He had two part time jobs on the go and hadn't missed a day of the course. Ian noticed Nick too and swung round to him angrily, "How come you're always so calm-nothing ever seems to affect you!"

Then Nick dropped the bombshell. He had begun planning for the Access course nearly a year before he started it. He had sat down over the course of weeks and months writing down anything that could threaten his progress through Access and university. Then for everything he'd written down he devised a way to deal with it – in some cases several alternatives. He'd even planned his finances as far as his final year at university.

"It wasn't rocket science," he said modestly," but I was determined that once I started, nothing was going to stop me." Meeting a girl friend? Covered. Getting her pregnant? Covered. Losing his job? Covered. He'd realistically written down the event of the death of his frail dad in Ireland…. Covered.

Very few have so long to plan; but you can anticipate certain things cropping up. Finance is an obvious one. Be absolutely methodical about how you will put food on the table and a roof over your head. Maybe you're lucky and have a well-paid working partner, or maybe you live with mum and dad. In all these cases you can plan for a lot of the monsters and banana skins. You'll probably never encounter them, but if you do, by planning ahead they will have minimal impact on your studies.

12

The good news is that the UK Government have set up and this year modified the Advanced Learner Loan system. Originally set up to give loans to the over 24's as from August 2016 the loans became available to Access students 19 or over. There is no credit check. Like the student loan for university study it does have to be repaid (to the Student Loans Company); but only if you are earning over £21000. But be aware that if you withdraw or are withdrawn from the Access course before completion, your College will undoubtedly pursue you for immediate repayment. So don't think that because the loan is there you can throw caution to the wind and take a punt. Incidentally, new legislation is under consideration which may change the basis of loan to mirror that of the **Postgraduate Loan** terms. You will need to clarify this when applying.

Also, remember that most Access students have their ups and downs but nothing serious enough to stop their studies.

Apart from financial implications there are other unexpected matters to be aware of. Sometimes friends perceive you differently once you start an Access course. You no longer fit into that comfy pigeonhole slightly below them.

> Becky was one of the younger members of the Access group. At 16 following a viral infection she'd become disabled by ME (Myalgic Encephalopathy) and dropped out of school. At 19 she enrolled on Access and worked hard. So I was surprised when she came to me one day in tears, "I've got to leave the course!"

> She would not say why, but a friend disclosed that her boy-friend had started undermining her. Questioning why she needed a degree when he would support her. It came down to a straight choice, him or the course.

> After talking with her very supportive mates on the course she decided to explain to him how much this meant to her, and also how much he meant. That she wouldn't want to give either up. He wasn't impressed.

Unfortunately the stress of this triggered a return of Becky's ME and she had to withdraw from the course. Her boy-friend almost immediately left her for someone else. Happily, Becky's ME was much less severe this time and tailed off. She was allowed to rejoin and complete the Access course the following year, went to university and graduated and is now a senior social worker.

Becky's case was one of the very rare but extreme ones. A college might get one or two Becky's in a five year period. The best strategy is to not make your plans to enrol a state secret, despite the temptation to "wait and see" how it pans out, "just in case". Friends and family do need to understand the huge demands this will make on your 'spare' time. For your part you need to be very sensitive to the effect this will have on them.

# Overall structure of the Access Diploma course

There's a lot of detail now- you might find it easier to look at the <u>Key Terms section first</u>!

Access courses are administered or accredited by an external organisation called the <u>Awarding Body</u>.

Access courses are called unitised courses. That means the course subjects are split into a number of sections or <u>units</u> – in the same way that A levels, degrees and a lot of other modern qualifications are. Each unit is assessed separately and is worth three, six or nine <u>credits</u> depending on the amount it covers.

The national regulations specify that you must accumulate a total of sixty credits across all your subjects. No more, no less. If you look at the following diagram, you will see that forty five of your credits have to be from graded units. When you complete the assessment for each unit the tutor will give you a <u>grade</u> for that unit, Pass, Merit or Distinction.

## Overall structure of a typical Access Course

Each block represents one unit of study
The numbers 3,6,9 are the number of credits
you are awarded for passing the unit

| | | | | 9 |
| | | | | 6 |
| | | | | 6 |
| | | | | 6 |
| | 3 | | | |
| 3 | 3 | 6 | 3 | 6 |
| 3 | 3 | | 3 | |

Maths(Units 1 -2)   English Units 3,4   Research Project   Psychology (Units   Science(Units 7-11)
                                        Unit 5             6,7)

Ungraded units                    Graded units

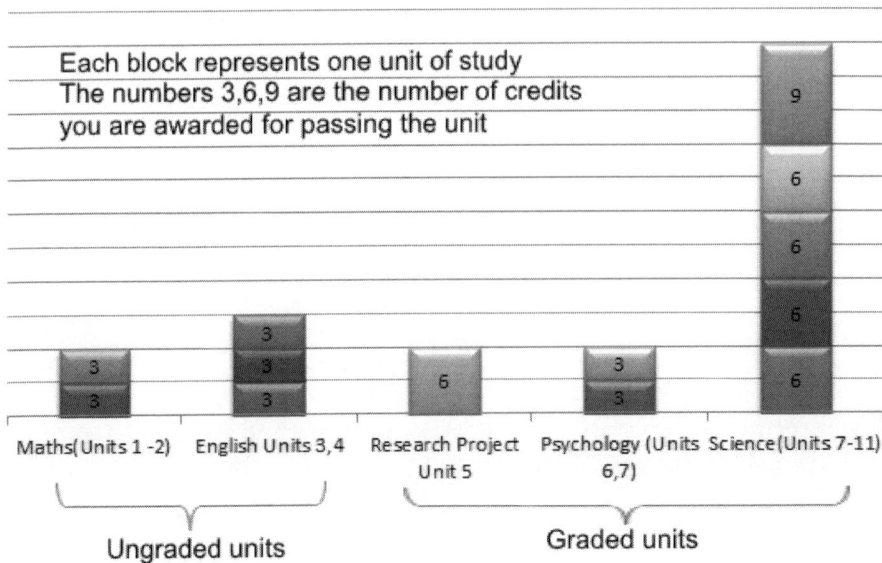

Note that when you finish the course your diploma will show individual grades for each unit. No overall grade is given. In the real thing, the Units will have names rather than "Unit 1".

Steve was an excellent student who went on to complete a first class honours degree in biology after his Access course. Here is an extract from his Access academic profile.

| Unit Title ---> | READING/WRITING | SPEAKING/LISTENING | RESEARCH SKILLS | CELLS | NUTRITION & DIGESTION | HOMEOSTASIS | GENETICS/REPRODUCTION | INTRODUCTORY PHYSICS | DEFENCE & IMMUNITY | CHEMISTRY | ADVANCED MATHEMATICS | PRACTICAL SCIENCE SKILLS | INDIVIDUAL SCIENTIFIC INVESTIGATION | MICROBIOLOGY | MUSCULOSKELETAL SYSTEM | NERVOUS SYSTEM | Total Credits Achieved | DISTINCTION GRADE | MERIT GRADE | PASS GRADE |
|---|---|---|---|---|---|---|---|---|---|---|---|---|---|---|---|---|---|---|---|---|
| No. of credits ----> | 3 | 3 | 6 | 3 | 3 | 3 | 3 | 3 | 3 | 3 | 6 | 6 | 6 | 3 | 3 | 3 | Credits | GRADE ANALYSIS | | |
| NIXON, STEVE | D | D | D | D | M | D | D | D | D | M | D | D | D | D | D | D | 60 | 54 | 6 | 0 |

You can see that Steve passed all his units for the sixty credits. In the last three columns on the right you can see he did so with fifty four Distinctions and six Merit credits. (This was before the current forty five credit limit on graded units came in)

His intended university had already told him they required at least thirty credits at Distinction in science, so he was home and dry.

**Units and credits**

The most important part of units for you is the Assessment criteria. The diagram shows a typical unit (this is an example which has not been validated or used).

**UNIT TITLE:   Introducing Clinical Pharmacology (1)**
**LEVEL:   Three**
**CREDIT VALUE:   3**
**UNIT CODE:**

This unit has Three learning outcomes.

| LEARNING OUTCOMES | ASSESSMENT CRITERIA |
|---|---|
| The learner should be able to: | The learner can: |
| 1 Understand basic factors in clinical drug administration | 1.1 Review some key factors in determining a useful level of a drug in the bloodstream (eg: dose and/or routes of administration and/or absorption and distribution and/or metabolism and excretion) |
| 2 Describe the way that named drugs achieve their effects | 2.1 Compare respectively the use of two or more named drugs against two or more named pathogens<br>2.2 Compare the use of two named drugs against a single named part or system of the body<br>2.3 Give one or more examples of possible negative effects for the drugs named for 2.1 or 2.2 may occur |
| 3 Interpret a scenario involving the use of clinical drugs | 3.1 Analyse the factors in a scenario involving the use of a named clinical drug |

From your point of view, you need only concern yourself with the right hand column. These criteria statements will be tested through assessments. You may be given more than one assessment to do for a three credit unit. Needless to say you should be given class input unless the assessment asks you to research a topic. The next chapter tells you more about assessments.

By the way, don't be fooled by those who say "Access is an easy route instead of A levels". The pass boundary for Access is 100%. If you miss just one of the hundreds of criteria, you cannot pass (though you may be allowed the chance at further assessment, which may be capped at pass). With A levels, so long as you get around 40%, you pass. I've had A* A level students top up with Access for entry to medicine and they have found it really tough.

Incidentally, you will find when you go to university you are more confident, better prepared, more organised and more resourceful than the vast majority of A level students. Good Access students are always among the top performers at university.  I know this is true because I have had hundreds of past Access students tell me so over the years. So hold your head high!

# Preparing and starting your course

## Preparation

Things to get ready for the course.

Not a lot. That's right, you don't need to up the limit on your credit card. The Access course will give you more academic work in 8 months than you have ever dreamed was possible. So you don't need to add to the burden. A marathon runner doesn't go out and run 26 miles just before the real marathon starts! But like the marathon runner you can get yourself ready to go!

## Pre-course reading.

For goodness' sake don't rush out and buy all the textbooks you'll need for the next 4 years! Remember, you don't even know what the unit criteria are yet. There are some low cost book suggestions for courses with science in (that's most Access courses) at the end of this book. Like this one, they are aimed specifically at returners to study.

The best preparation is to start broad. Often overlooked, but there are marvellous 30 minute programmes on Radio 4 every week covering just about every area in a very listenable and up to date manner. There's bound to be something there for you. Go to the Radio 4 website and click on Categories to find what's on for you. TV programmes are less easy-they are long and not designed for you to take in while you do the ironing, make a cup of tea. They demand your 100% attention. Frankly, you will probably find Radio wins hands down over TV!

Broaden your reading too. Pick up the odd "serious" magazine or journal that you haven't tried before. Drink it in. A bit braver, look at the free Open University OpenLearn website. There's a huge range of very short introductory programmes there. No assessment, you can just dip in and out.

**Make a friend of your computer.**

At college you will probably have the pick of hundreds of computers to work on. You have probably also got access to one at home; iPhone, iPad, Kindle, PC, lapbook, notebook, tablet, the list grows by the year. At college and also at university, access to a computer to do your work on is an absolute must. That's a *reliable* computer and a reliable internet connection.

You also need to regard it as your willing workhorse. Make sure that you know how to use it to search for information. Ask a friend to show you round some of the basics of searching, word processing and emailing. It is more straightforward now than ever before.

By getting confident now with your computer, you will have equipped yourself well for the course.

**Limbering up for Access**

Doing an Access course is mentally draining – especially so at the very start of the course. When you are mentally drained you feel tired physically too. It works the other way round – and you can use that to your advantage. So establish a pattern to get yourself physically active. Something as simple 20-30 minutes brisk walking 2-3 times a week is a good start. You can work it into your college day too at lunchtime or in a spare period between sessions.

Get your eyes checked! You will be doing more reading and close work than you have done in your life. The last thing you want is difficulty in reading the tutor's screen, or something you've been given to work on.

Eye strain leads to atrocious, distracting headaches. You can address it easily.

Diet. Seriously – pay attention to your diet. Make sure you get plenty of balanced meals. B vitamins are important for nervous function so plenty of vegetables … and unless you are vegan don't neglect some red meat or liver each week. Fish, especially oily fish is said to be beneficial. If you are vegan or vegetarian, you already know about B rich alternatives from things like mushrooms, yeast extract and fortified foods.

Grog. Watch the grog. You don't need to give it up! But overdoing it in the week means missed sessions and poor performance the next day at college. Bingeing at the weekend ruins the one time most students set aside for doing more lengthy assignments. The same goes for recreational drugs.

Schedule. The secret of Nick's success lay in his planning. You need your Access timetable before you start so you can arrange things like childcare and transport. You may need to nag the college for it.

Here's the bad news. Your timetable may well be changed when you start the course. That's because colleges are under pressure to keep recruiting students. Sometimes they under or over recruit. Infuriating for you but it can happen. So like Nick, be ready with a plan B and C if changes in times will affect you!

**Stationery**


You do not need a huge amount to start the course. An A4 ring binder (cost about £1), a pad of A4 lined paper (£2.00) some coloured pens (roller calls or ballpoints, not felt tips!), a maths set (ie ruler,protractor,set squares,compass etc- £2 the lot). A calculator-though many students use their phones now.

Optional but useful are a little hole puncher and a stapler. Also some clear poly filing pockets to keep papers tidy. Note that when you complete your portfolio you'll have to take papers out of these.

iPads, iPods, laptops,notebooks are useful but not essential. As costs come down, more and more are appearing in class.

Don't bother with a Dictaphone for recording lectures. You will find that the days of long lectures are largely a thing of the past (dinosaur tutors excluded). In any case, the sound quality is always bad-its only on playback you realise how much background noise is going on; chairs scraping, people coughing, tutor um-ahing and moving to the other side of the room to answer someone's question. In quite a few cases you will find that enlightened tutors produce Podcasts of their sessions that you can download and listen to at your leisure. I also like to produce short (10 minute) videos where appropriate, summarising tricky topics. If you cannot attend due to the 'flu you will find Podcasts and Screencasts are a tremendous help to you in keeping up.

## The first term

Access tutors are people. And because people are different, so are Access tutors. So you may find some more approachable than others-it's a personal thing. One thing they all have in common is a commitment to mature students like you. Having said this you'll find they do it in different ways and with different styles. Some you love, some infuriate you, some scare the living daylights out of you.

Access students are people too! The first week or two can be terrifying! There is always at least one person who already seems to know everything and who tries to hijack the tutor's attention all the time. Experienced tutors will soon suss them out and make sure that everyone else gets their fair share of attention. There's an old proverb, 'Empty vessels make the most sound'. In a high proportion of cases, when the empty vessels put their first assessment in, the truth of the proverb is obvious to the tutor. In my experience, 50% of the empty vessels leave the course by Christmas, to go off and bore someone else. The other 50% settle down and become part of the group.

Your feet will barely have touched the college ground, when tutors start talking about you applying through UCAS for your university place. That's why it is so important for you to have done your research to pick out the right universities to apply for. You'll usually be expected to finalise your UCAS application before Christmas. Be prepared!

Where possible, go to university Open Days to get a feel for the different places and their surroundings and accommodation. Some 'sought after' universities are placed in really grotty areas! Remember too that universities put their best face on for visitors. I remember accompanying my daughter to a nice sounding London university's Open Day. As we got nearer and nearer there our hearts sank lower and lower at the dire surroundings. Inside the grounds it was different. High mellow brick walls coated with roses surrounded the campus. Polite well spoken security guards strolled the well mown lawns (albeit with German Shepherd dogs). Students lounged by a small lake. The hall of residence we were shown had sumptuous carpets, porter service, a plush common room. At the presentation, the Vice President trilled about the care for students, her door was always open, the safety of the campus, how the gates were locked every evening and so on.

The reality when my daughter did her degree was very different. No security guards on 24/7 duty with GSD's. No carpeted Halls of Residence or porter service - that was for wealthy international students only. The lake got rather smelly – especially after social events on the campus. The campus gates were never closed and you could drive in and out as much as you liked without being challenged. Oh, and the VP was never in; she was always partying it up at other universities. Despite that, there was never any trouble there, my daughter loved it and got hooked on London life for good.

You will also get your first taste of being assessed on the units. Which bring you to the next section.

# Assessments/assignments

Don't be afraid of them! They must stick strictly to the criteria. You should be given a written (or electronic) Assessment Brief. The Brief should carry details of what you are expected to do and when the deadline is. They will also tell you what you need to do to gain higher grades of Merit or Distinction. If you do not understand what you need to do, ask the tutor. They will not dictate the answer to you but they are required to explain exactly what the task is.

When you tackle an assessment, you must obviously look at the tutor's instructions. But check those criteria too. The criteria contain words called "Action Verbs" and you need to do what they say. Look at the section on Action Verbs now.

Strictly speaking, assessments should not go beyond the criteria action verb. However a tutor may decide to give you scope to gain Merit or Distinction by encouraging you to "explain" even if the criteria say "describe" for Pass.

Note that under Government pressure there is an increasing emphasis on SPAG (spelling,punctuation and grammar). Access courses will teach you these skills but it's up to you to use them. Forget to spell check at your peril!

## Getting the best grades in assessments

It is natural to aim for high grades. Whenever students get graded work back, they are all looking over each other's shoulders. It's easy to get demoralised when others get a merit or distinction and you get a pass. Don't. Always remember you are part of a group rather than part of a team. Your strongest competitor is you. Your most critical friend is you.

You are not aiming at the same level as your classmates – you are aiming at your own personal best every time.

Some students like to work in little support groups on assessments. Facebook groups abound in Access classes. Where an assessment involves a series of individual questions or sub tasks they may each work on a different one then come together for a final run through. Nothing wrong with that at all-it will happen at university too.

But ….. make sure that the actual work you submit builds on that group activity. I've noticed time and time again that the highest scoring students are the ones who have double checked other people's work and extended it through some extra research on their own account.

Two final words about every assessment that you are given. Start early.


**With a Google here, a Google there, here a click, there a click everywhere a click-click**


Google is great. Wikipedia is wicked. Internet research is always being updated; it is worldwide and instantly available.

Compared to maybe 20 years ago, doing research is amazing. No more ordering from some far flung library miles away. It's fast using the internet too, oh so fast! Much quicker and easier than trawling through the index of a book and then the impenetrable text. Quicker too because you can bookmark or you can select and printout or save the information you want.

Most tutors encourage use of the internet these days. Though there are still some dinosaurs who say there's no substitute for book and journal research and the internet should be avoided. Hopefully not on your course.

You got some hints on using IT and Google in the chapter about <u>Preparing for your course</u>. Google and other search engines are excellent at giving you answers – the "what?" But they won't immediately give you the "why?" It's the "why?" that you will need to give in your Access work. Recent research (e.g. See Stonetemple Consulting website at https://www.stonetemple.com/rich-answers-in-search [accessed 04/08/17]) suggests that good search engines give 'Information rich' answers 19% of the time. Meaning you need to dig deeper to get the "why?" in around 80% of queries.

Sometimes it will save you time if you cut out the middle man. For example, if you have to find something out about a particular topic, why not go straight to the online version of the professional journals? "The British Medical Journal", or "The Practicing Midwife", for instance. You will get reliable, up to date information directly related to UK research.

So, next time you do a search and get an answer, make sure you can explain "why?" As a tutor I'll sometimes say to a student in a one-to-one tutorial, "That's a really good answer," and they preen themselves, "But I'm a bit foggy-can you explain what it means?" Answer, "Er….. what's the question again?"

Watch out too for just copying and pasting from the internet-even with a bit of changing. More and more tutors are asking for work to be submitted to them online through an anti-plagiarism checker such as Turnitin™. colleges and universities are very strict on plagiarism nowadays. It will cost you dear.

Remember too, tutors want to see *your* work, not a rehash of someone else's. So even if you add references after the copied work, you won't get full or any credit.


Apart from those cautions – embrace the internet!

# New Year – a short aside …..

When you get asked, "What do you want for Christmas?" there are two answers. Well three if you include 'a new computer', but I will ignore that one.

Present 1: this is where you wheel out that list of very expensive textbooks you have got from the Access tutors in the first term. These will be the ones to take you right through Access, right through university and beyond.

Present 2: your bright new outfit for January and February. And that includes males and females. Why? Because January and February are the doldrums' days. It's dark when you go to college and dark when you come home. A large depression is continually over the UK – centred on your house. Well actually on you. It's when the assignment load starts to pour over you like magma bubbling from a volcano. It's when you are depressed waiting to hear from universities.

When you go to college every day everyone else seems grey, like 1990s politicians. But if you put on some brighter clothes, lively colours, it will make you feel good because it brightens other people up and they in turn will cheer you up. Try it. And rest assured that before long the university offers will start to trickle through and everything will be good again.

# The end of the course

By the time Christmas arrives, you will probably have several pieces of assessed work in your ring binder which is starting to bulge anyway.

It's time to start assembling your portfolio. Your portfolio is a collection of all your assessed pieces of work along with the assessment briefs and tutor feedback. It won't fit into your ring binder. What you need is an A4 Level Arch file. You can buy them for anything between £1 and £8. The trouble with the cheaper ones (and some of the expensive ones too) is that the hoops soon become strained and have the habit of dropping everything on the floor. Usually in a puddle. Unfortunately you can only discover their durability by buying one.

You will receive detailed instructions about how to organise the paperwork in your portfolio file. However here is a common format.

The first page will be an index. The second will be a sheet listing your achievement for the whole course. Then you will need a series of labelled card dividers, one for each subject. Each section will then be further separated by dividers into the various units for that subject. Into each subsection you pop your assessed work and details of the grading you have achieved for the unit.

There will probably be times when the Course Manager asks you to leave portfolios for something called Internal Moderation. This is where a different college tutor reviews the marking of work by the original tutor and decides if it is consistent. This ensures fair grading for every student.

Usually twice in the year, the red carpet will be rolled out for the External Moderator. External Moderators are independent professionals, usually highly experienced Access tutors or university lecturers from outside your college. They are appointed by the Awarding Body. The External Moderator also wants to choose and inspect samples of students' work.

Remember that they are not directly checking you, they are checking your college's procedures.

On the External Moderator's final visit, usually in June or July, extensive samples are checked for the second time and a formal Final Award Board is convened. At this meeting, every student's performance is scrutinised by senior professionals and a formal decision taken to issue or not issue the Diploma.

Usually, the college will then send written transcripts and confirmation of the Diploma to the student. You should take a copy, but send the original to your selected university, so they can confirm your place. In due course you will receive the Diploma document from the awarding body.

And then? Well then, you've got a few weeks over the summer to relax, before you move onto the next chapter at university!

# Key Terms

**Assessment/Assignment** – Strictly speaking the criteria are tested through assessment tasks set by the tutor. However very often tutors use the term 'Assignment' instead of 'Assessment'. Just go with it. Either way you need to do it to pass! Assessments may be written work or answering questions or Case Studies or timed test questions or presentations – the list is endless!

**Awarding Body** – an external organisation effectively empowered by the relevant Government body to award Access Diplomas.

**Credits** – each unit has a value counted by the number of credits. The credit value of a unit is an all or nothing value. With a 3 credit unit you either get 3 credits or nothing.

**Criteria** – units are made up of a set of statements called criteria. These state what you must be able to show you can do in order to pass the unit. All a unit's criteria have to be met to pass the unit. No part marks are available.

**Graded and ungraded** units – Depending on your performance, a graded unit will be awarded at Pass, Merit or Distinction. Universities use the credits on graded units in an equivalent way to A*. A, B, C on A level courses. The grading does not affect the number of credits. In other words a 3 credit unit gets you 3 credits at Pass or, Merit, or Distinction.

**Lates/late submission** – tutors are likely to cap any late submission of work at pass – if they accept it at all.

**Levels** – the vast majority of Access units are at Level Three which is immediately pre-degree level. They will also be at the Foundation Year level of degree courses that have Foundation Years. Level Two is rarely available, and then only for ungraded units.

**Modules** – the term has fallen out of use for many Access courses now. You probably won't hear it. Sometimes you will hear it used instead of the term unit. Sometimes tutors use it to describe a cluster of units in a particular subject. Sometimes they just mean a text written to support a unit. If it seems important, ask a tutor to clarify.

**Plagiarism** – a serious offence which can result at best in you having to repeat work, or modules (at extra cost), at worst be kicked off the course. Plagiarism is where you offer work from somebody else as your own. 'Somebody else' could be a book, journal, internet, or another student even if you both agreed to work together on somethin

**Referral** – if you have to resubmit any assignment or part of it(see resubmission), but still do not pass you may qualify for a "referral". This means that your work will not be passed but will be referred to the powers that be. They may set you a further piece of work which will be capped at pass.

**Resubmission** – The tutor may set you a fresh piece of work to cover anything you have not met in your first submission of an assessment. Under the current revised regulations your resubmission will then be graded in the same way as any other submission.

**Units** – each subject is divided into shorter block of study called units. So English is quite often made up of two units. One may be a Speaking and Listening unit, the second a Reading and Writing unit.

Click here to go back to more details about the assessment of Access courses.

# Action Verbs in assessments/assignments

When doing assessments for a tutor look out for these words in the criteria and also the assignment brief. Not doing what they say will affect your success. The list is not exhaustive-there are lots of terms. Ask the tutor when unsure.

**Assess** – Means you should offer a balanced judgement of the topic, reinforced by relevant facts. [Example, "Assess the arguments for more home care to be available for the elderly".

**Compare** – Means what it says. Forget your own prejudices. Make matching statements for each of the topics. Both similarities and differences. [E.g. "Compare the benefits of swimming and running as forms of exercise" The response might include, "Both improve cardiovascular performance, however whereas running can lead to impact joint injuries, swimming does not because …. On the other hand the impact of running helps build bone density much more effectively than swimming where the body is supported…."

**Contrast** – Is similar to compare except that you need to highlight the differences.

**Define** – Give a succinct one sentence statement describing the meaning of the term. [E.g. "Define digestion", answer " Digestion is the progressive mechanical and chemical breakdown of food into individual molecules"]

**Describe** – Means what it says. In a graph like this you would say, "In the first 120 seconds there was a steady fall in heart rate from 190 to 170 beats per minute. Then heart rate fell more quickly to 90 bpm at 360 seconds, with an even sharper fall to 70bpm at 420 second….."etc. You don't gain any marks for trying to explain why in a "describe" question.

# Heart rate adjustment post-exercise

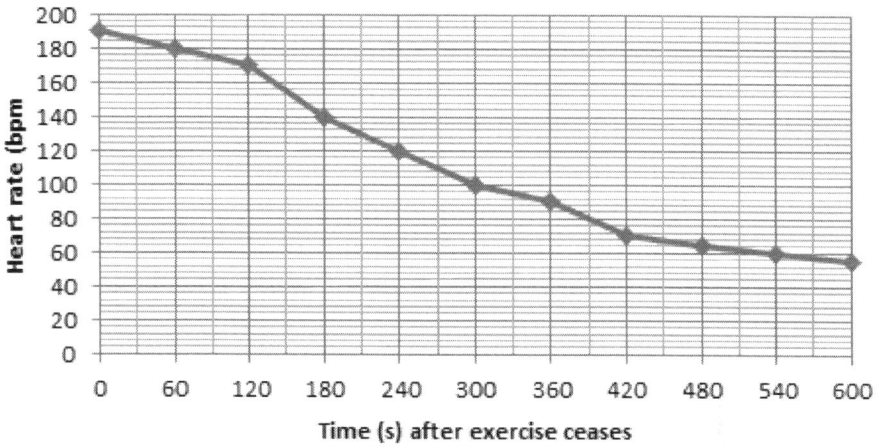

Heart rate (bpm) vs Time (s) after exercise ceases

**Explain** – Means what it says. Just describing gets you no marks. "Heart rate rises to supply extra oxygen to muscles for aerobic respiration during exercise. This leads to oxygen debt. The heart rate remains high for the first 360 seconds so that extra oxygen can reach the muscles. As the level of oxygen is restored, heart rate drops more sharply (from 360 seconds) reaching resting rate after 600 seconds." (Don't worry about understanding this- but you get the idea?)

**Evaluate** – a favourite with some Access tutors. Also may be interpreted differently by them. It *should* mean weighing up the pros and cons of something in order to come to a judgement. Check (if this is) what the tutor wants.

**Examine** – Investigate something closely and in detail. "Examine the increase in death of Ash trees in the UK". Examine questions *may* not require you to make a judgement.

**Explore** – Typical where you need to research something. More to do with finding out, without necessarily needing the level of detail in "Examine" questions. Again, check this with the tutor.

**Investigate** – Another research based type question. This is one where you may need to pin the tutor down as to how far they want you to go in terms of analysis.

**Outline** – Means produce a description setting out the key points of the topic. Should not involve any further discussion (unless tutor asks for it!)

**Review** – Survey the results of some research (yours or of others). Make a judgement as to what is reliable evidence and what gaps remain.

**Summarise** – Produce a short round up in your own words of whatever the topic is.

# Other books for Access students

1. Basic Introductions to Biology – Cells tissues and circulation (in e-book format OR as a paperback)
2. Basic Introductions to Biology - Book 2 Digestion, blood sugar and diabetes
3. Basic Introductions to Biology- Book 3 Kidneys, structure and functions
4. Basic Introductions to Biology - Bacteria Viruses and Fungi
5. Basic Introductions to Biology - Disease and immunity: An introduction to defence,immunity and pharmacology
6. A basic introduction to chemistry

22804236R00023

Printed in Great Britain
by Amazon